The Words & Wisdom of

of

Will Rogers

R. Scott Frothingham

CONTENTS

CONTENTS

About The "Words & Wisdom" Series

Inspired by the works of his great-great grandfather Edward S. Ellis, R. Scott Frothingham has published the "Words & Wisdom" series featuring American historical figures -- including Abraham Lincoln, Benjamin Franklin, Theodore Roosevelt, Mark Twain and others. Frothingham explains:

> Growing up, I loved the living room in my grandmother's house in Rye, NY. The room featured a fireplace, a grand piano and two floor-to-ceiling built-in bookshelves taking up the entire walls on either side of a French door to the 3-season screened porch.

> Those shelves were entirely filled with books written by her grandfather "Grampy Ellis". A good number of those books were read aloud to me, and as I grew older, I read many to myself; always amazed that one of my relatives had been such a prolific author and delighting in the exploits of Deerfoot and other tales of frontier adventure.

> One of the first books I read from Ellis' later life -- when he had shifted from dime novels to more serious work -- was *Thomas Jefferson -A Character Sketch*. Fondly remembering the discovery of that book, I thought I would celebrate Edward S. Ellis's love of America, history and biographies by giving readers a slightly different look at some important Americans and the events surrounding their lives, by letting those historical figures speak for themselves.

Thus, the "Words & Wisdom" series was conceived --
featuring selections of the actual words of historical
figures -- to offer a better understanding of the people
behind the beloved icons and notable events we are
presented in brief during grade school.

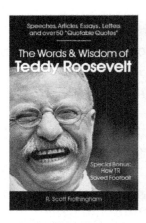
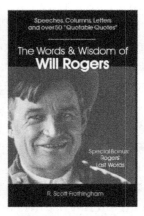
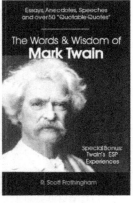
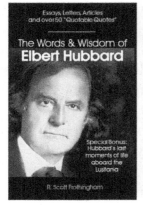

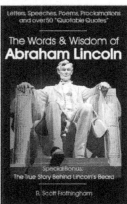

"The Words & Wisdom of Will Rogers" is dedicated to Edward S. Ellis' granddaughter Katharine Taylor Woods and her children, Ellis's great grandchildren, Katharine Ruth Woods Frothingham and Allan Scott Woods

As a "**Thank You**" for purchasing this book, here is a **FREE** eBook: *"Thomas Jefferson – A Character Sketch"* – get your copy at: **www.EdwardSEllis.com/Thank-You-(TJ).html**

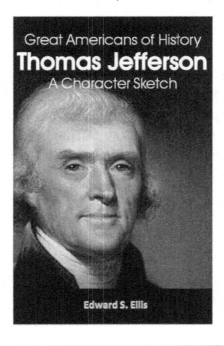

Publisher's Preface

Will Rogers was perhaps the best loved American of his age and was one of the world's best-known celebrities in the 1920s and 1930s. Born in Indian Territory (now Oklahoma) in 1879, William Penn Adair "Will" Rogers was part Cowboy and part Indian. About ¼ Cherokee, he quipped, *"My ancestors didn't come over on the Mayflower, but they were there to meet the boat."*

A star of the circus, vaudeville, Broadway stage, and radio, Will was the #1 male box office leader at the movies from 1933 until his death (ahead of Fred Astaire, Clark Gable and James Cagney). He was also the most widely read and frequently quoted internationally syndicated columnist of his day with about 40 million readers (the population of the US at that time was about120 million).

Nicknamed the "cowboy philosopher," Rogers was known for the folksy charm he brought to his wryly humorous way of looking at the world. Although his observations were presented as a simple country boy's musings on the imponderables of life, they had an intellectual undercurrent that made people think while they were laughing. With charm and magnetism, Rogers perfected a homey, confiding way of talking that made his listeners feel that he was talking straight to them.

Although Rogers was a well-informed and skilled commentator, his persona emphasized his simple, rural background and lack of formal education with earthy anecdotes and a "down home" style that allowed him to poke fun at controversial topics like prohibition and government programs and satirically skewer public figures from politicians to gangsters, and do it in a way in which no one was offended.

> *I use only one set method in my little gags, and that is to try to keep to the truth. Of course you can exaggerate it, but what you say must be based on truth. Personally I don't like the jokes that get the biggest laughs, as they are generally as broad as a house and require no thought at all. I like one where, if you are with a friend, and hear it, it makes you think, and you nudge your friend and say, "He's right about that." I would rather have you do that than to have you laugh—and then forget the next minute what it was you laughed at.*

Rogers was a prolific writer (it is estimated that he had more than two million words printed in various media) and his writings are valued for, among other things, the insight they provide into the concerns and opinions of the United States during the tumultuous decades of the 1920s and 1930s.

In this book, you will find a number of such articles and broadcasts including observations on key events such as the Great Depression, Prohibition, the situation in Cuba, the recognition of Russia, the hoof-and-mouth epidemic and the Dustbowl; as well as observations on important figures including Woodrow Wilson, Helen Keller and Henry Ford. Included is perhaps his most famous broadcast known as the "Bacon and Beans and Limousines" Speech.

Throughout his career, Rogers offered political commentary, jabbing constantly at Congress. In fact, he gave the members of Congress credit for supplying him with comic material: *I don't know jokes; I just watch the government and report the facts.* Herein you will also find two satire pieces, 1 nominating Henry Ford for President and 1 suggesting that he, Will Rogers, has the right qualifications to be the Vice President.

You will also get a glimpse of the private Will Rogers in letters he wrote to his wife and his eldest son, plus a moving letter of condolence to the widow of his dear friend Charles Russell.

Also included is a "before and after", showing you Rogers' notes for a speech followed by the transcript of the actual speech; and the interesting (and funny) Rogers' response a "cease and desist" letter from the lawyers for the publishers of the "Literary Digest" against Rogers' "The Illiterate Digest". In his trademark folksy manner, Rogers charms and jokes his way through his response, effectively defusing the situation, *"...now I want to inform you truly that this is the first that I knew my Title of the Illiterate Digest was an infringement on yours as they mean the direct opposite, If a magazine was published called Yes and another Bird put one out called No I suppose he would be infringeing. But you are a Lawyer and its your business to change the meaning of words, so I lose before I start,"*

Will Rogers is an interesting original on many levels, I hope you enjoy this compilation of words and wisdom from this intelligent, colorful and entertaining observer of the America of the 1920's and1930's.

R. Scott Frothingham
Vienna, VA

NOTE: Throughout this book you will find spelling and grammatical errors. That's because we have purposely not corrected Rogers' original text (e.g., Rogers often wrote "didn't" as "dident" and used commas where a period is typically called for), including typos that were in the original (e.g., in the telegram to the *Washington Post,* he misspelled his last name "Roegrs").

Quotable Quotes from Will Rogers

Before we get to the long-form speeches and articles, let's take a look at some of the great "sound bite" quotes attributed to this "larger-than-life" figure from the past.

"Worrying is like paying on a debt that may never come due."

"Never miss a good chance to shut up."

"When you find yourself in a hole, quit digging."

"If there are no dogs in Heaven, then when I die I want to go where they went."

"Even if you are on the right track, you'll get run over if you just sit there."

"Too many people spend money they haven't earned, to buy things they don't want, to impress people they don't like."

"Why not go out on a limb? That's where the fruit is."

"All I know is just what I read in the papers, and that's an alibi for my ignorance."

"You know horses are smarter than people. You never heard of a horse going broke betting on people."

"Everyone is ignorant, only on different subjects."

"The difference between death and taxes is death doesn't get worse every time Congress meets."

"Everything is funny as long as it is happening to somebody else."

"There are three kinds of men. The ones that learn by readin'. The few who learn by observation. The rest of them have to pee on the electric fence for themselves."

"We can't all be heroes because somebody has to sit on the curb and clap as they go by."

"There are two theories to arguing with a woman. Neither works."

"A man only learns in two ways, one by reading, and the other by association with smarter people."

"Do the best you can, and don't take life too serious."

"Common sense ain't common."

"Rumor travels faster, but it don't stay put as long as truth."

"The road to success is dotted with many tempting parking spaces."

"Ten men in our country could buy the whole world and ten million can't buy enough to eat."

"Don't let yesterday take up too much of today."

"It's not what we don't know that hurts. It's what we know that ain't so."

"Buy land. They ain't making any more of the stuff."

"Most men are about as happy as they make up their minds to be."

"Heroing is one of the shortest-lived professions there is."

"Liberty doesn't work as well in practice as it does in speeches."

"What the country needs is dirtier fingernails and cleaner minds."

"Personally, I have always felt that the best doctor in the world is the Veterinarian. He can't ask his patients what is the matter...he's just got to know."

"When you're through learning, you're through."

"Things ain't what they used to be and probably never was."

"Plans get you into things but you've got to work your way out."

"Good judgment comes from experience, and a lot of that comes from bad judgment."

"There are men running governments who shouldn't be allowed to play with matches."

"If you can't identify it, don't stick it in your mouth."

"Never kick a cow chip on a hot day."

"Take the diplomacy out of war and the thing would fall flat in a week."

"If you want to be successful, it's just this simple. Know what you are doing. Love what you are doing. And believe in what you are doing."

If advertisers spent the same amount of money on improving their products as they do on advertising then they wouldn't have to advertise them.

Ohio claims they are due a president as they haven't had one since Taft. Look at the United States, they have not had one since Lincoln.

"Half our life is spent trying to find something to do with the time we have rushed through life trying to save."

"An onion can make people cry, but there has never been a vegetable invented to make them laugh."

"If you feel the urge, don't be afraid to go on a wild goose chase. What do you think wild geese are for anyway?"

"The best way out of a difficulty is through it."

"People who fly into a rage always make a bad landing."

"When ignorance gets started it knows no bounds."

"It's not what you pay a man, but what he costs you that counts."

"Get someone else to blow your horn and the sound will carry twice as far."

"Lettin' the cat outta the bag is a whole lot easier 'n puttin' it back in."

"There is nothing so stupid as the educated man if you get him off the thing he was educated in.

"I've got my epitaph all worked out. When I'm tucked away in the old graveyard west of Oologah, I hope they will cut this epitaph: 'Here lies Will Rogers. He joked about every prominent man of his time, but he never met one he didn't like.' I'm so proud of that, I can hardly wait till they can use it."

Speech to Bankers

In this speech, Rogers skewers the banking industry. The origins of the speech are unknown, but it appeared on a Victor Records recording released in 1923. Rogers might have been speaking before the American Bankers Association annual convention of 1922.

Loan sharks and interest hounds—I have addressed every form of organized graft in the United States, excepting Congress, so it's naturally a pleasure for me to appear before the biggest.

You are without a doubt the most disgustingly rich audience I ever talked to, with the possible exception of the bootleggers' union, Local No. 1, combined with the enforcement officers.

Now, I understand that you hold this convention every year to announce what the annual gyp will be. I have often wondered where the depositors hold their convention. I had an account in the bank once, and the banker, he asked me to withdraw it. He said I had used up more red ink than the account was worth.

I see where your convention was opened by a prayer, you had to send outside your ranks to get somebody that knew how to pray. You should have had one creditor there; he'd have shown you how to pray. I noticed in the prayer the clergyman announced to the Almighty that the bankers were here. Well, it wasn't exactly an announcement. It was more in the nature of a warning. He didn't tell the devil, as he figured he knew where you all were all the time anyhow.

I see by your speeches that you're very optimistic of the business conditions of the coming year. Boy, I don't blame you. If I had your dough, I'd be optimistic too.

Will you please tell me what you all do with the vice presidents the bank has? I guess that's to get anybody more discouraged before they can see the main guy. Why, the United States is the biggest business institution in the world. They got only one vice president. Nobody's ever found anything for him to do.

You have a wonderful organization. I understand you have 10,000 here, and what you have in federal prisons brings your membership up to around 30,000. So goodbye, paupers. You're the finest bunch of shylocks that ever foreclosed a mortgage on a widow's home.

The Dust Bowl

The following is an excerpt from a monologue Will Rogers delivered to a live audience on April 14, 1935, a few months before his death. It addresses the US "Dust Bowl" of the 1930's in which the plains states were choked by dust caused by years of poor agricultural practices and years of sustained drought.

Any old great civilization that they've ever gone and dug up, they go down and find two or three layers all buried there in the dust. And they've all been covered up because of the ploughed up ground that shouldn't ever been ploughed up in the first place and the trees cut down that shouldn't never been cut down anyway.

You know, we're always talkin' about the pioneers and what great folks the old pioneers were. Well, I think if we just stop and look history in the face, the pioneer wasn't anything in the world but a guy that wanted something for nothin' - that's about all they were. He was a guy that wanted to live off everything nature had done. He wanted to cut a tree down that never did cost him anything...but he never did plant one. We're just now learning that we can rob from nature the same as we can rob from an individual. All the pioneer had was an ax and a plough and a gun and he went out and lived off nature. Least he thought it was nature he was livin' off of, but really, it was future generations he was livin' off of!

Now, remember here a couple of years back when Roosevelt suggested plantin' millions of trees all across the dry regions? He said, "Ever so many miles, we'll put a row of trees clear across the country!" Well, the Republicans had one of the best laughs they've had since 1928 when they read that. "Imagine the government going into the tree planting business! What a nut idea!" Well, it was so nutty that it would be about ten to fifteen years before they'd be *compelled* to do it - that's how "nutty" it was!

Another one of Roosevelt's ideas was when he took the young boys off the roads and off the streets and put 'em into these CCC camps and had'em all planting these little trees. The press all had a big laugh off that, too - called 'em "saplin' planters" and said "Look at these youn kids - they got 'em all plantin' saplings!"

Well, if the saplin' planters had started in about the time the Republicans took over the government from Grover Cleveland, why, today, we'd be able to see the sun!

"Bacon and Beans and Limousines" Speech

Rogers gave what became one of his most famous speeches when he and President Herbert Hoover were booked together for a special radio broadcast on October 18, 1931 to restore confidence in the economy. Officially named the "President's Organization on Unemployment Relief Broadcast" the speech became known as the "Bacon and Beans and Limousines" speech, even though Will never used any of those three words in the talk.

> NOTE: This speech was incorporated into the 1990s Broadway show, THE WILL ROGERS FOLLIES and was performed by singer/actor Mac Davis at the 1992 National Democratic Convention.

Now don't get scared and start turning off your radios. I'm not advertising or trying to sell you anything. If the mouthwash you are using is not the right kind and it tastes sort of like sheep dip why you'll just have to go right on using it. I can't advise any other kind at all. And if the cigarettes that you are using, why if they don't lower your Adam's apple, why I don't know of any that will. You will just have to cut out apples, I guess. That's the only thing I know.

Now, Mr. Owen Young asked me to annoy on this program this evening. You all know Mr. Owen D. Young. You know, he's the only sole surviving wealthy Democrat, so naturally when a wealthy Democrat asks me to do anything I have to do it, see?

Well, Mr. Young, he's head of the Young Plan. He's the originator of the Young Financial European Plan. He's head of the Young Men's Temperance Union, and originator of Young's Markets, and Young Kippur. And was the first Democratic child born of white parents in Youngstown, Ohio.

He started the Young Plan in Europe. That was that every nation pay just according to what they could afford to pay, see? And, well, somebody else come along with an older plan than Young's plan, and it was that nobody don't pay anybody anything, and course that's the oldest plan there is. And that's the one they are working under now. That's why we ain't getting anything from Europe.

So when Mr. Young asked me to appear why I said, "Well, I'm kind of particular. Who is going to be the other speaker? Who else is on the bill with me?" And he said, "Well, how would Mr. Hoover do?"

Well, I slightly heard of him, you know, and I said, "Well, I'll think it over." So I looked into Mr. Hoover's record and inquired of everybody, and after I had kind of thrown out about two-thirds of what the Democrats said about him why I figured that I wouldn't have much to lose by appearing with Mr. Hoover, so I'm here this evening appearing on the bill with Mr. Hoover. So now I expect you won't hear any more of "Amos and Andy"; it will just be Hoover and Rogers from now on.

Now we read in the papers every day, and they get us all excited over one or a dozen different problems that's supposed to be before this country. There's not really but one problem before the whole country at this time. It's not the balancing of Mr. Mellon's budget [Secretary of the Treasury]. That's his worry. That ain't ours. And it's not the League of Nations that we read so much about. It's not the silver question. The only problem that confronts this country today is at least

7,000,000 people are out of work. That's our only problem. There is no other one before us at all. It's to see that every man that wants to is able to work, is allowed to find a place to go to work, and also to arrange some way of getting more equal distribution of the wealth in the country.

Now it's Prohibition, we hear a lot about that. Well, that's nothing to compare to your neighbor's children that are hungry. It's food, it ain't drink that we are worried about today. Here a few years ago we were so afraid that the poor people was liable to take a drink that now we've fixed so that they can't even get something to eat.

So here we are, in a country with more wheat, and more corn, and more money in the bank, more cotton, more everything in the world; there's not a product that you can name that we haven't got more of than any other country ever had on the face of the earth, and yet we've got people starving. We'll hold the distinction of being the only nation in the history of the world that ever went to the poor house in an automobile. The potter's fields are lined with granaries full of grain. Now if there ain't something cockeyed in an arrangement like that then this microphone here in front of me is, well, it's a cuspidor, that's all.

Now I think that perhaps they will arrange it, I think some of our big men will perhaps get some way of fixing a different distribution of things. If they don't they are certainly not big men and won't be with us long. Now I say, and have always claimed, that things would pick up in '32. Thirty-two, why '32? Well, because '32 is an election year, see, and the Republicans always see that everything looks good on election year, see? They give us three good years and one bad one. No, no, three bad ones and one good one. I like to got it wrong. That's the Democrats does the other. They give us three bad years and one good one, but the good one always comes on the year that the voting is, see? Now if they was running this year why they would be all right. But they are one year late. Everything will pick up next year and be fine.

These people that you are asked to aid, why they are not asking for charity, they are naturally asking for a job, but if you can't give them a job why the next best thing you can do is see that they have food and the necessities of life. You know, there's not a one of us has anything that these people that are without it now haven't contributed to what we've got. I don't suppose there is the most unemployed or the hungriest man in America that hasn't contributed in some way to the wealth of every millionaire in America. It was the big boys themselves who thought that this financial drunk we were going through was going to last forever. They over-merged, and over-capitalized, and over-everything else. That's the fix that we're in now.

Now I think that every town and every city will raise this money. In fact, they can't afford not to. They've got the money because there's as much money in the country as there ever was. Only fewer people have it, but it's there. And I think the towns will all raise it because I've been on a good many charity affairs all over the country and I have yet to see a town or a city ever fail to raise the money when they knew the need was there and they saw the necessity. Every one of them will come through.

Europe don't like us and they think we're arrogant, and bad manners, and have a million faults, but every one of them, well, they give us credit for being liberal [meaning generous].

Doggone it, people are liberal. Americans, I don't know about America being fundamentally sound and all that after-dinner hooey, but I do know that America is fundamentally liberal.

Now I want to thank Mr. Gifford, the head of this unemployment, thank Mr. Young, and I certainly want to thank Mr. Hoover for the privilege of being allowed to appear on the same program with him because I know that this subject is very dear to Mr. Hoover's heart and know that he would rather see the problem of unemployment solved than he would to see all the other problems he has before him combined. And if every town and every city will get out and raise their quota, what they need for this winter, why it will make him a very happy man, and happiness hasn't been a steady diet with our President. He's had a very tough, uphill fight, and this will make him feel very good. He's a very human man. I thank you. Good night.

The Illiterate Digest

The following, including the exchange of letters (genuine) are the dedication of Rogers' 1924 book "The Illiterate Digest".

Most Books have to have an Excuse by some one for the Author, but this is the only Book ever written that has to have an Alibi for the Title, too. About 4 years ago, out in California, I was writing sayings for the Screen and I called it the Illiterate Digest. Well one day up bobs the following letter from this N. Y. Lawyer. It and the answer are absolutely just as they were exchanged at that time.

WILLIAM BEVERLY WINSLOW
LAWYER
55 Liberty Street,
New York, N. Y.

Nov. 5th, 1920.

Will Rogers, Esq.,
c/o Goldwyn Studios,
Culver City, Calif.

Dear Sir:

My client, the Funk & Wagnalls Company, publishers of the "Literary Digest" have requested me to write to you in regard to your use of the phrase, "The Illiterate Digest," as a title to a moving picture subject gotten up by you, the consequence of which may have escaped your consideration.

For more than two years past it (my client) has placed upon the moving picture screen a short reel subject carrying the title "Topics of the Day," selected from the Press of the World by "The Literary Digest. "This subject has achieved a wide popularity both because of the character and renown of "The Literary Digest" and through the expenditure of much time, effort and money by its owners in presenting the subject to the public. "The Literary Digest" is a publication nearly thirty years old, and from a small beginning has become probably the most influential weekly publication in the world. Its name and the phrase "Topics of the Day" are fully covered by usage as trademarks as well as by registration as such in the United States Patent Office.

During several months past your "title," "The Illiterate Digest" has been repeatedly called to our attention and we are told that the prestige of "The Literary Digest" is being lowered by the subject matter of your film as well as by the title of your film because the public naturally confuse the two subjects. We are also told that exhibitors are being misled by the similarity of titles and that some of them install your subject in the expectation that they are securing "The Literary Digest Topics of the Day."

It seems to me self-evident that your title would scarcely have been thought of or adopted had it not been for our magazine and for our film. If this were not the case the title which you use would be without significance to the general public.

I have advised the publishers that they may proceed against you through the Federal Trade Commission in Washington calling upon you to there defend yourself against the charge of "unfair competition," because of your simulation of their title, or that they can proceed against you, the producers of your film, its distributors and exhibitors in court for an injunction restraining you from use of the title, "The Illiterate Digest."

Before, however, instituting any proceedings in either direction they have suggested that I write directly to you to see if your sense of fairness will not cause you to voluntarily withdraw the use of the objectionable title.

Unless I hear favorably from you on or before the first of December, I shall conclude that you are not willing to accede to this suggestion and will take such steps as I may deem advisable.

Yours truly,

(Signed)

William Beverly Winslow.

WBW/als

REPLY:

Los Angeles, Cal.,
Nov. 15, 1920.

MR WM BEVERLY WINSLOW,

Dear Sir,

Your letter in regard to my competition with the Literary Digest received and I never felt as swelled up in my life, And am glad you wrote directly to me instead of communicating with my Lawyers, As I have not yet reached that stage of

prominence where I was commiting unlawful acts and requireing a Lawyer, Now if the Literary Digest feels that the competition is to keen for them—to show you my good sportsmanship I will withdraw, In fact I had already quit as the gentlemen who put it out were behind in their payments and my humor kinder waned, in fact after a few weeks of no payments I couldent think of a single joke. And now I want to inform you truly that this is the first that I knew my Title of the Illiterate Digest was an infringement on yours as they mean the direct opposite, If a magazine was published called Yes and another Bird put one out called No I suppose he would be infringeing. But you are a Lawyer and its your business to change the meaning of words, so I lose before I start,

Now I have not written for these people in months and they havent put any gags out unless it is some of the old ones still playing. If they are using gags that I wrote on topical things 6 months ago then I must admit that they would be in competition with the ones the Literary Digest Screen uses now. I will gladly furnish you with their address, in case you want to enter suit, And as I have no Lawyer you can take my case too and whatever we get out of them we will split at the usual Lawyer rates of 80-20, the client of course getting the 20,

Now you inform your Editors at once that their most dangerous rival has withdrawn, and that they can go ahead and resume publication, But you inform Your clients that if they ever take up Rope Throwing or chewing gum that I will consider it a direct infringement of my rights and will protect it with one of the best Kosher Lawyers in Oklahoma, Your letter to me telling me I was in competition with the

Digest would be just like Harding writing to Cox and telling him he took some of his votes,

So long Beverly if you ever come to California, come out to Beverly where I live and see me

Illiterately yours

WILL ROGERS

When I sent him my answer I read it to some of the Movie Company I was working with at the time and they kept asking me afterwards if I had received an answer. I did not, and I just thought, oh well, there I go and waste a letter on some High Brow Lawyer with no sense of humor. I was sore at myself for writing it. About 6 months later I came back to join the Follies and who should come to call on me but the nicest old Gentleman I had ever met, especially in the law profession. He was the one I had written the letter to, and he had had Photographic Copies made of my letter and had given them around to all his Lawyer friends. So it is to him and his sense of humor, that I dedicate this Volume of deep thought. I might also state that the Literary Digest was broad-minded enough to realize that there was room for both, and I want to thank them for allowing me to announce my Illiteracy publicly.

A Letter to Betty Blake Rogers

"The day I roped Betty Blake was the best catch of my life."
Rogers met Betty Blake the Oologah, Indian Territory train station. They were friends on and off for 8 years and married November 23, 1908 when Rogers was 28. There was a lot of correspondence between the two both before and after the marriage, this example is from a few weeks after they were married.

To Betty Blake Rogers
25 April 1909
Louisville, KY

Sunday, 10:30 a.m.

My Own Dear Wife,

Well hon, here I am and say but it is lonesome and I sho do miss you all the time and more than ever now since I got here and it is as lonesome as the D_____

Well old hon, after you left I got off the train and Dr Bushyhead was out on the Platform waiting for me and I was with him up to 11_____oclock when my train left. we just sit around down at the Drug store and talked. then on the train Joe Chambeers was going up to Chelsea to the dance that night. Got to St. Louis it was about noon train a little late. Went down on the stage at the American Theatre and saw all the boys and at 2 oclock out to the Ball Game   saw the Worlds Champion Chicago team play St. Louis and beat them too   then back and sent you a lot of Music   address to Dick so you would be sure to get it. sent the Real Silvers Rag. learn it good so you can play it when you come   couldent get the world to Loving Rad. then had Supper. also sent clem that one piece Silvers Rag, too. then back on the stage behind and saw part of the show at the American and left at 10:10 P.M. on the Southern Railway   sent you a wire from Depot   did you get it. got here at 7 a.m. and there is no Hotels in this town but this big one so I finally just come here and got a nice little single room for $1.25 a day. *not* with a bath of course and I can only have it till Tuesday as they have a big Convention of some kind but I will find me one by that time and I dont mind moving as I have nothing but comb and brush and a collar. it is a ~~beautiful~~ nice hotel   nothing like the Baltimore though

Buck had got in yesterday all O.K.

It is nice and warm here. I am billed second up next to the Headliner. The Country Kids and that Kid act from Newark you remember that was with me are the Headliners. I close the show. open this afternoon   that act is the only one that I know personally

Well I'll bet that you are just getting ready to have one glorious feed for dinner today and I sho would like to be there too and after dinner we would go for a good old drive but I'll bet it wouldent be as good as the one we took at home would it   I enjoyed that more than any drive I ever had. and we were looking at *our own* things then.

I know you had a good time with Sandy. hope he got to go home with you and you all will be having a big reunion today. Give my love to Mamma and Dick and all of them and tell them how I wish I was there and that I will be before long

Old Honey Bug I got that Dandy picture of you just right here in front of me and it sho does make me wish for you. I feel *"awful"* lonesome today   its been such a long old day and it is not noon yet   maby it will be better after I get to work. I got me a lot of Sunday papers and I will read till Show time   Now if they have any dances and card parties you just go to all of them cause I want you to have a good time and you must get you some new clothes too   I will send you the money   I want you to look nice   Get Tom Morgan to Show you the Variety. last weeks of the Denver shows. and see what it saysabout your old Hussy.

Well my Sweetheart Wife I must close cause you might want this long a letter all the time. With all the Love of your old Husband   I sho do miss you and love you a lot.

You only,

Billy.

American Foreign Policy

In this weekly article Rogers offer thoughts on Cuba, American foreign policy, revolutions and empire building ... all in his friendly, folksy style.

DON'T GET EXCITED

Well all I know is just what I read in the papers. I been pretty busy trying to keep peace in Cuba. I know Mr. Roosevelt dident want any armed trouble with them and he was doing the right thing, but we still have a lot of that old domineering spirit in us. We just can't forget our size and our strength and we do kinder like to go prowling off into some outlandish place with a bunch of marines and settling somebody's troubles for 'em.

You see, we have always figured that Cuba was a kind of stepchild and while it was big enough to earn its own living and was not living at home anymore, why we still had the right to step in and advise. You see, the child has grown up but we haven't. We still think in terms of Nicaragua, of Hati, of San Domingo, of Mexico, all these we have been in some sort of messes with. We meant well, but we just do love to nose about. We can't seem to bear to seeing anything going on without us at least offering advice.

Advice can get you in more trouble than a gun can. I just don't want somebody telling me how to run my business, or my country. I want to ruin it myself without outside aid, and that's especially true of these Latin races. The minute there is any trouble in any Latin American Country, that should be the tip right there for us to crawl in a hole and not even be allowed to poke our head out till it was all over, for as sure as we could see it we would either be in it or offering advice. We can't help it, it's just second nature with us. We mean well, but the better we mean the worse we get in.

Let the Argentine come up and settle it. They speak the same language, and they are a big influntial country. Let Mexico advise Cuba, they have no stepfather treaty with 'em. You see there is where we got in wrong, we retained a clause in our Treaty with 'em where we had a kind of a string tied to 'em yet so while they got their liberty from Spain, there was still a second mortgage given to us which we still hold and shake over their head every once in a while. We just sit by the hour at home and abroad and tell "Why don't England give India her freedom. What's England got to do with Canada. Australia should be a free country, why should she have a string on South Africa."

That's all fine, but the minute an Englishman reminds us of Cuba, or the Phillipines we are up in arms and come back at 'em. "Well that's different we are only in there to help them out. We get nothing out of it." And the Englishman says, yeah, and we can't make him see it our way. Ain't people dumb when they won't see things your way. That's why we have always thought Englishmen have no sense of humor they just won't laugh at our jokes as much as we think the jokes demand.

Another thing about all this trouble in Cuba, Boliva, Paraguay, and all those is that folks forget that a Latin American Country must have so much revolution and wars anyhow. They don't look on a revolution as being such a terrible thing like we do.

They are a people that don't get much excitement and a good revolution is a sort of relaxation for 'em. Now take the Argentine, they had peace for a long time and finally it began to get on their nerves and they couldent stand it any longer so they just broke out.

Well I was down there since then, and the humiliation of the thing was terrible to 'em. Not that they had had a revolution, that was really a picnic, but what they hated more than anything was that the rest of the world would class them as "Just another South American revolutionist Country." In other words they had lost face (as the Chinese say) if there was some way where every once in awhile they could have them a nice little home talent revolution without the rest of the World knowing it. Why it would be fine everybody would be for it. But it hurts their credit with the rest of the world to have the news get out.

A revolution kinder comes under the heading of amusement as well as a nessisity with them in all those countries and we shouldent get so excited about it. We take everything too serious. The greatest contribution to peace in the World would be an international clause, "Any Nation can have a nice local revolution any time it sees fit, without any outside aid or advice from America or England."

Rogers Addresses the Depression

Rogers' writings are valued for the insight they provide into the concerns and opinions of the United States during the tumultuous decades of the 1920s and 1930s. In this article he comments on the variety of solutions for the Great Depression and offers the thought that the only cure is the next generation.

NOW TO SOLVE THE DEPRESSION

Well all I know is just what I read in the papers or what I gather from pamphlets that people send me solving the World situation. Somebody is sure doing good, that is in the printing line. Every guy that's got a scheme, racket, idea, or hallucination, gets it put in pamphlet form and while the letter R comes pretty late in the alphabet, they must have me mixed with the letter A.

I am the first to receive this Depression Solver. Now it's not that I don't appreciate it, I do, I think it's mighty nice of 'em to think of me, but I wish they would think of me—well I wish they would just think of me.

In case anyone happens to ask you, this is a pretty tough Depression, and it's going to take more than a pamphlet to dig us out. I don't even believe a whole book will do it, and there is just about as many books coming in as there is pamphlets. Maybe pamphlets gradually grow into books, maybe they start out as just a barber shop argument. The fellow gets more words and he issues one of these little dodgers, or throw aways, then he feels that what the dodger lacked was a little more explanation. Then the dodger becomes a pamphlet. Now it ain't much of a jump from a pamphlet to a book, provided you get out the book yourself. As the depression increases why your solution gradually gets longer, so it's beginning to be realized that maybe the thing won't really be solved with not even a book, but maybe two to six volumes. So when the volumes commence coming in, even if the postage is paid, I am going to dive right off one of these Santa Monica mountains.

I believe that's what's the matter with this depression, everybody wants to solve it and nobody wants to work at anything else. I believe if it was announced that it couldn't be solved, why there would be enough people released from solving it. They would go back to working on nobody but their own problems, and maybe first thing we knew we would be doing pretty good. In fact I think just the announcement of the fact that it couldn't be solved would be a blessing. Everybody feels better when you really know even the worst. It's this uncertainty of not knowing that's a worrying us more than the actual discomforts of it. I will bet you one thing, I bet you in the next Presidential race, you won't get candidates coming out saying they can fix it. They have learned their lesson. The most that will be said in the next campaign platform of either party will be: "Now boys, we are going to try and check it, but we are not saying we will, but we will promise you this, we are not going to let it spread any more than we can possibly help."

You see the way I figure this thing will end is that the depression won't be solved. It will just remain with us and as a new generation grows up why they won't be used to anything else and they won't mind it. Wait till the ones who lived through the Coolidge era are all dead. You see any person that lived through those times just can't get it out of his head. The World was spoiled for him anyhow.

So what must be done is grow up more children, and do what we can to get us old ones to drop off. We can't remember anything but the days when all we had to do to get anything under the sun that we wasn't used to, or didn't need, was to just nod your head in the affirmative, and give the fellow the address where to send it. The thought of money changing hands was considered rather vulgar, everything was on time. If we was to actually have good times, why we still wouldn't welcome it if we had to pay for anything and not get it on credit.

But these young ones coming along. The old car will be worn out, the radio gone, and a hundred and one other things he won't know anything about, he will only buy what he needs, and will pay for it. So you see the depression won't end till we grow a generation that knows how to live on what they got and never knew anything else.

The Notes and The Speech

Rogers' speeches and performances always sounded spontaneous, but he often wrote and re-wrote notes. In April of 1930, Rogers was invited to speak at the dedication of a statue in Oklahoma. To get a feel for his process, below you will first see his notes, and then you will see a transcription of the actual speech (as written by a newspaper reporter).

Notes for a Speech at the Dedication of the Pioneer Woman Statue
22 April 1930
Ponca City, OK
Right off we will get it settled why I am here, I am here to pinch hit for the Governor in case he is impeached before hisspeech is oevr,
Thats why all these people camoe they thougyt they would see an unveiling and an impeachment combined,
they take the census from the impeachments,,
We know enough on this Guy but we haven't got anybody to take his place
It looked like rain this morning, in fact rain would have done us more go than a Statue, The Rep- cant even give us rain,
The Democrats did better than that ~~they~~ we was all wet all the time they was in,
Pat Hurley,
Calvin Coolidge,
Virginia and her Statues
Hoover

Bronze instaed of marble. Jackson. Day dinner. Old Oklahoma instead of the strip.

London Conference the Kings speech

Looks like an osage payment, Theapymnets of the cherokkeesss,

Takes a pretty broad minded wife to allow her husband to come clear to Oklahoma to help take the clothes off another woman,

We are here today to help out the Pioneer woman,

We are here to day to pay her honor, she dident vote, she cooked, anf How.

That's the Woman I want to help out is the old time Woman,

The new Woman I want to help the men out,

Theold time women must have been wonderful, In fact any woman thats living in a differebt age from ours must have be en wonder ½ful.

The Corsets, Thats an address book, The Boys got too claen a face to be

She is looking into the future she's got dumb democratic Marlins, fine spirit and originality, - most Oil men would have erected one to themselves, or to John D Rockeffeller,

The old sooners ½that settled this country, passed through Claremore, we sold this for it was no good,

You have to strike oil to pay your taxes,

We are going to erect a Statue in Claremore to Bell Star;

Article in an Unknown Newspaper
(clipping found in Rogers' files)

23 April 1930

WILL ROGERS MADE LONG
TRIP TO TALK TO 'HOME FOLKS'

Will Rogers, an honor gures for the Tuesday ceremony, made his flying trip from Los Angeles to Ponca City to talk to the "home folks." At least, that was his answer when someone on the speakers' stand warned him, in the midst of his talk, that he was standing too far from the Microphone.

"Oh, I don't care," he answered, waving a hand. "I can talk to the United States any time. I'm here today to talk to home folks."

Rogers followed the other speakers on the program and opened with: "Now, that the applesauce and 'boloney' is all over we'll state a few facts about this affair. The pioneers here sneaked in ahead of the gun. You had to be a crook or you wouldn't he here. If you'd waited until the gun for the run you wouldn't have got any land.

Skipping from that to the census, he declared: "Oklahoma takes its census by having a man stand outside the capitol and take the names of the governors as they come out. We've got enough on this fellow (nodding toward Governor Holloway standing near him) to impeach him, but we haven't found anyone else who will take the job.

"Pat Hurley is making good as a secretary of war, as long as we have no war. He's trying to start one now. And he'll fight in it if we have one. The republicans will have one to solve the unemployment problem.

"It was might nice of President Hoover to take time off from appointing commissions to open this program. He used to lin in Pawhuska and we use to have a clock in Claremore he'd come over to see what time it was.

"Coolidge and I usually open these things. He was coming here but Mr. Marland kicked kicked on paying his expenses. I wanted him to come here but he couldn't find where it was. Besides, he didn't carry the state and Hoover did, so he spoke to us.

"I'm a colonel on the governor's staff, he says. I hoped the state would make that appointment so that it would be continuous. I have to be changing jobs so often.

"This is the biggest crowd in Oklahoma since the Jack Walton barbecue. We'll go far to eat in this state.

"This statue – I'm all wet about it. I wrote out my notes, all about a statue covered in marble and here it's in pewter or something. Now I've got to rub out this speech and write another.

"I want to pay tribute to my wife. It takes a bright-minded wife to let a man fly 1,500 miles to take some clothes off a woman.

"The artist has done a wonderful job here. It's the first time I've seen a long skirt in years. And that's the keenest face I ever saw on an Oklahoma boy. Wonderful statue, no joke, and no comical things about that. And she's got on corsets. The kind, remember, that used to come up when you were sitting around at parties, come up so that the girls couldn't see over them.

"Everybody is running for something today. If I tried to take home all the campaign literature the airplane wouldn't fly.

"But I'm here to act a fool for you and I'll come anytime. And I'm going to erect a statue at Claremore to Belle Starr."

Letter to Will Rogers, Jr.

Even at the height of his popularity, Rogers considered himself a family man and often wrote to his children Will, Jr., Mary and Jim when he was traveling. This letter of October 20, 1928 is typical of Rogers' family correspondence. Will and wife Betty were at a New York hotel while the children stayed at the family ranch near Pacific Palisades, CA and he writes to teenaged Will, Jr. about family news and theatrical stories and offers parental advice.

My Dear Son.

This should reach you on your Birthday, You are seventeen years old, It don't seem that you can be that old, but we got to go by the records and you mama's memory, we are mighty proud of you, and think you are a fine Boy, and we want you to just stay a fine Boy,

We got a nice letter from Mr Lawlor and he spoke very highly of you, Now that's pretty fine to impress amn [a man] like that, I am tickled to death with your Polo record, for I think it is a fine game and will physically do you a lot of good, I want you to do all you can in any game that will develop your shoulders and strength,

How are you coming in school?. Mt [Mr.?] Wills will be going back in a few days and you must start with him two or three times a week, he will show you all that is being done in the show,

My little dancing goes over great, the little stunt with Dorothy and I down near the finish of the show is the biggest hit in the show, I have two comedy songs that go fine, One [with] Andy Tombs)he is the fellow that used to do Gallager and Shean with me in the Follies) we have on dress suits and are barefooted, and ist [it's] a scream, We never look at our feet or let on that we are not fully dressed,

The Show looks like on of the Hits of Broadway,
I am more anxious for Xmas to come than you all are, we will have a big time,

I hear Jim is tak ng [taking] up his trick riding, I am sure glad of that, I wish he would bring up a pony, Old Punpkin and have Hank Potts help him on it, it will make his shoulders and back so much stronger,

I have a great act for Mary and when I get home,
Now you must work hard, and keep right up in all your classes, and be nice and polite, and considerate of all the older people you meet and they will all like you for it,

I am enclosing seventeen Dollars, and here is a couple of clippings, we sill send you all of them when we get them together, All the papers treated us fine, Mama wants to give you for your Birthday, a Charge account at the Book store, so you can goand get any of the books that you want, Beebe's, or when America comes of Age. or any reference books, tell Aunt Dick to arrange it for you,

Write me and tell me all about the horses, How is Cowboy coming, have you ridden him yet, and Panther, is his jaw OK. Mama and I get mighty lonesome for you all, a Hit in New York don't hardly pay for what else we miss I tell you,

But we know you are all doing fine, and learning , so stick to it, That's what I am trying to do here, Its not just waht I would like to do, But all of us have to do things, that are best for us, and thats what you are all having to do in school now,

Well we are going over to the Theatre now, love to all of you,

You are more to your old Daddy than all the so called successes in the World, Happy birthday Son, kisses and hugs for all of you,

Daddy.

Fish Eggs and Firewater

On November 16, 1933, President Franklin Roosevelt ended almost 16 years of American non-recognition of the Soviet Union. Rogers offered the following comments on the re-establishment of formal diplomatic relations.

NOW WE RECOGNIZE WHISKERS, CAVIAR, BORSCH AND VODKA

Well, all I know is just what I read in the papers and what I hear from the boys that are talking. There never was a time when as many people had their heads together like a quartette. And they ain't all singing the blues either. There is an awful lot of not only hope, but a whole lot of confidence in people in their country. We have recognized Russia, but you would be surprised at the amount of people that are not going there to settle. Their big importation is caviar, (that's a kind a gooey mess of fish eggs that I suppose is without doubt the poorest fodder in the world) but it costs a lot and the rich just lap it up, like they do grand opera when they can't understand a line.

But as long as a fish has gone to the trouble to lay the eggs, (especially when they go away up in Russia to lay 'em) — we got fish here that must lay eggs, but we don't pay any attention to them, any more than we would to an American lecturer. The eggs our fish lay are just home talent. They are just a kind of a local egg. But if the same fish went west in Russia and layed those same eggs, why then they become important eggs. Instead of just a setting of meal. Now if you got a good meal coming, what's the idea of eating something before it. If it was good it would spoil your meal, for you would eat too much of it, and if it's not any good it will spoil your meal anyhow. So it just looks like we recognized Russia in order to give the Russian fish that wanted to lay eggs a chance.

Now of course there is some parts of the world where there is certain fish that are better, but you wouldent hardly think there was anywhere eggs are better, especially fish eggs. But of course being a Democrat and not a caviar eater, I don't know anything about it. I like the cocktails though that they put with 'em, that's about all I can see in caviar. the next big importation that we will get from Russia outside of a setting of these eggs is a thing called Vodka. Now vodka is just as different from a fish egg as a man's ideas that got a post office, from the one that dident get one. Vodka is a fluid, but it's what could rightly be classed as a deceptive fluid. It's as harmful a looking thing as a nice goard full of branch water. But there the comparison stops. It's made from fermented Russian wheat, corn, oats, barley, alfalfa, or Jimpson weed, just which ever one of these they happen to have handy. Now any of 'em as I say is the ground work. Then they start adding the ingredients.

Potato peelings is one of 'em, then Russian boot tops. You know over here we have the tops of carrots and onions and all those; well over there they all wear these high boots, so you just take the tops of as many Russian boots, as you can get when the men are asleep, you harvest 'em just above the ankle, you shock 'em up like wheat, then bring one of those Russian carts along where there is a high yoke up over the horses neck you know a Russian horse always looks like he is going under an arch de triumph. The next ingredient (the Russians always deny this to me, but I have always believed it's true) is the whiskers, they say that they don't put 'em in vodka, that they are only used in that soup called borsch.

Now then you add all these things then it's got to ferment. Well it don't take long for anything to ferment in Russia. They are a nation that can start stewing before you know it. Now then you get this vodka built up, and if it's concocted by a good architect, it's just as clear and innocent looking as a stein of gin. That is it is before you start sampling it. Well when you do your eyes begin expanding, and your ears begin to flopping like a mule's. It's the only drink where you drink and try to grit your teeth at the same time. It gives the most immediate results of any libation ever concocted, you don't have to wait for it to act. By the time it reaches the Adams Apple it's has acted. A man stepping on a red hot poker could show no more immediate animation. It's the only drink where you can hit the man that handed it you before he can possibly get away. It pays quicker dividends than any libation ever assembled. You don't go through that period where people say, "Silas is getting tight." Say brother, when Silas lifts that glass, Silas is not getting tight, Silas is out. It's a time saver. It should especially appeal to Americans, there is nothing so dull in American life as that period when a drinker is just at that annoying stage. He is a pest to everybody, but vodka eliminates that, you are never at the pest period.

So we haven't started to realize the benefits we got from recognizing Russia, till the caviar and the vodka start rolling in.

Rogers and Helen Keller (part 1)

Here is a letter from Helen Keller to Rogers regarding, among other things, a copy of her book "Midstream" that she had sent him. That letter is followed by a letter of response from Rogers that included a contribution to the American Foundation for the Blind.

April 1, 1930.

Dear Will Rogers:

I am going to heap coals of fire upon your amazingly wise head by writing you a letter --- a long, reproachful letter --- an audacious begging letter. Ever and ever so long ago I sent you "Midstream," --- a large book, a perfectly respectable book, and you have never deigned to say if you received it. Well, I forgive you, as I can't possible hold a grudge against one who gives me pleasure every day of my life. If I didn't read your morning paragraph in the "New York Times," I should doubt if the sun was shining.

Since you seem able to help everybody who gets into trouble, I am going to deposit my budget of problems for your consideration. I have been spellbound by your cleverness in finding ideas for those who haven't any. You have made suggestions for the farmer, the Democratic Party and the Naval Limitation Conference. You have supplied the U.S. Senate with a fair substitute for brains and found sticking-plaster for the unseemly breach between President Hoover and the Republican Party. Compared with all these problems, mine is simple.

For five years I have worked like a beaver (not a mythical beaver either) to raise two million dollars, so that the American Foundation for the Blind may have adequate funds to serve all classes of the blind contructively (sic). Up to date the Endowment Fund has reached about seven hundred thousand dollars. (This does not include the one hundred thousand from the Conrad Hubert Fund because we have not received it yet.) I am now engaged in a determined effort to reach the first million mark before June. When this is accomplished, we have reason to believe that Mr. John D. Rockefeller Jr. and other large donors will make substantial contributions. A gift of twenty-five thousand --- a wonderful surprise I received Christmas Eve from a friend in Philadelphia who wishes his name not to be mentioned --- emboldens me to anticipate the realization of my life-dream -- to open doors of usefulness to thousands of blind people.

The fixed idea in my mind is not merely the achievement of my goal, but the thought that when the Foundation has that two million dollars, the blind will be no longer beggars at the door of charity. Until then we cannot create a right attitude towards them on the part of the public, and the blind suffer from the wrong attitude of the world towards them more than from blindness.

Another reason for my eagerness to complete the Fund as soon as possible is, that my beloved teacher, Anne Sullivan Macy, who has been my companion and helper during forty-three years, is rapidly losing her sight, and I cannot tell how long she will be able to give me the assistance in my work upon which I have always counted. Your heart will interpret for you her anxiety and my own sorrow. I have had the sweet joy of helping to save others' sight, and I can do nothing for the one nearest to me! You have made a splendid success of your life, and I know you will not want me to fail now when my heart is sad, and all about me is uncertainty and the dark.

You are the magician of words. You know how to open hearts as well as the lips of laughter. You have probably heart (sic) how the Egyptians believed that if one pronounced the name of a god in a certain ingratiating way when asking for a boon, it would be granted forthwith, no matter what the purpose of the petition was. Alas! my speech is halting and unbeautiful, it would not win favor in the Court of the Gods. But with you it is very different, dear Will Rogers. Because you have the magic, will you not say something that will bring a degree of independence and normal happiness to the blind of America? A few golden words from you would mean more to the sightless than a handsome contribution in dollars.

If this letter is too long, and you haven't time to read it, all right, I greet you anyhow as a scatterer of sunshine and good-will among men.

Sincerely yours,

Helen Keller

Beverly Hills Hotel and Bungalows
Beverly Hills, California
May 27, 1930

REPLY:

My dear Miss Keller:

Now what a fine Heel I turned out to be. Here I read your whole book plum through, (and by the way its the first one I ever remember doing that). When I got through reading what these Cuckoo Republicans have done the day before, why my day is about over. But I read yours and enjoyed every minute of it. Now about that Fund I am trying to figure what to say that might attract some attention, cause it sure is a good thing and I will get to it as soon as I get it through my old bone head the way to get at it.

Here's my little dab, its not much on the way to two million but I just don't want Rockefeller to be the only one in the R's.

When you coming out to see us Movie Folks. (sic) I will use you in a Picture if you come out. Give my love to that wonderful Teacher of yours. Drop me a line and send me some literature of that undertaking of yours.

If you can be fortunate enough to keep Mr. Hoover from appointing a Committee to help you raise that fund I believe you will make it.

You know I think you and I will be better friends if we dont (sic) meet, they tell me you can feel of ones face and tell how they look. I'll stay out of your clutches.

With the usual admiration of an American for their most remarkable Women,

(My wife cant (sic) call that being too affectionate, can she)

Yours
[Signature]
WILL ROGERS

Rogers and Helen Keller (part 2)

Rogers writes about Helen Keller and a charity event in which he is participating.

A THOUGHT FOR CHRISTMAS

Well all I know is just what I read in the papers, or what I am fortunate enough to get in the mail, well this week we are doubly fortunate, for I don't believe I am betraying any breach of etiquette when I reprint a letter that I just received from the world's most remarkable woman, Miss Helen Keller. We often exchange some words.

"Dear Will: Here I come. This time all I want is the loan of your voice. The American Foundation for the Blind has produced and perfected what is called the talking-book. These books are reproduced on a machine which is a combination radio and phonograph. A book of about ninety thousand words can be recorded on a dozen discs, thus bringing to the blind the pleasure and satisfaction of reading by ear any time they choose. Instead of having to use the tedious method of finger reading or wait upon the convenience of others to read aloud to them. In addition to the talking book they will have a radio.

"These machines are sold to the sightless at actual cost. The Library of Congress is having a number of records made which it will loan through its various branch libraries for the blind, but unfortunately the vast majority of the blind can't afford the machines. During the last few years the British Broadcasting

Company has on Xmas afternoon each year made an appeal for funds to purchase radios for the blind of Great Britain, and over the period more than twenty thousand radios have been furnished. It has been suggested that a similar appeal in this country around Xmas time be made and might secure equally as good results for talking-book-machines.

"The Columbia Broadcasting Company has been approached in this matter, and will be glad to co-operate and give us time over their system. My job is to get some radio personalities to make the appeal. Rest assured that no precedent will be established, in regard to doing something outside your contractual radio obligations, since the blind are recognized as a class apart from all other handicapped groups. Be it said to the credit of humanity that no one would begrudge the blind a special service.

"I am writing this letter from the Doctors Hospital where I am staying near my dear teacher who is ill. She who has for almost fifty years been my eyes and ears is now quite in the dark herself, but her physician is hopeful of being able to give her back a little sight.

"Am making a similar request to Edwin C. Hill, Alexander Wollcott, and yourself. Day and time will be arranged if my three friends, or even one, will grant the request. With good wishes, yours sincerely, Helen Keller."

Now ain't that a wonderful letter, and what a wonderful thing that is for the blind, and in a telegram I just today received, the date has been set for January 16th, nine thirty to ten. (I imagine she means eastern time) and John McCormack is to sing. I have such fine and broad minded sponsors in my radio work, the Gulf Oil Company, that I don't even ask them permission in a case like this. They wouldent even expect it. Now what I am trying to do is to get this letter to you before Xmas, (in most places it will be printed on the Sunday before Xmas, so that will still give you a day to act). Your radio stores will know about it. The most I know of it is from this letter, and it's called a "Talking Book," a combination radio and phonograph. So you still have time to do a good deed, one of the most gratifying I know of.

Isn't that an odd thing about that marvelous teacher of hers being sightless? She is a remarkable woman, the combination of those two women, the tedious work, and devotion on both sides, I doubt if its parallel is in history. If any of you younger folks, or kids are not familiar with the case of this wonderful woman, Helen Keller, and her remarkable teacher, make your folks tell you about her, make your teacher give you a whole class hour's lecture on her, get one of her own books, "The Story of My Life" that describes her almost miracle life. It will be one of the legends of our country. People by the million are out of work, and millions of more are out of things they are used to, but when you think you can still see, you can hear, you can talk. Yet this wonderful letter was written by someone who was denied all these, and yet she was trying to use her talents to help ones whom she felt were more unfortunate than her. Remember get the radio for Xmas for some blind one, and then tune in on her programme on January sixteenth, thank you.

His Best Comedy Writers

Will Rogers' favorite target subject was the US Congress, "taking shots" at both Democrats and Republicans. As demonstrated in this article published June 8, 1824, Rogers credited Congress with supplying him with both events and funny lines.

Most people and actors appearing on the stage have some writer write their material. I don't do that. Congress is good enough for me. They have been writing my material for years.

I just got back from Washington, D. C (Department of Comedy). I had heard that the Congressional Show was to close on June 7th. I don't see why they are closing then. They could bring that same show with the original cast they have to New York, and it would run for years.

I am to go into Ziegfeld's new Follies, and I have no act. So I thought I will run down to Washington and get some material. Most people and actors appearing on the stage have some writers to write their material – but I don't do that. Congress is good enough for me. They have been writing my material for years and I am not ashamed of the material I have had. I am going to stick to them.

Why should I go and pay some famous author, or even myself, sit down all day trying to dope out something funny to say on the stage? No sir; I have found that here is nothing as funny as things that have happened. So I just have them mail me every day the Congressional Record. It is to me what the Police Gazette used to be to the fellow who as waiting for a haircut. In other words, it is a life saver.

Rogers in the Congressional Record

Rogers feigned great pride when he was quoted during a session of Congress (and thus his words were officially entered into the Congressional Record):

I feel pretty good about that; that's the highest praise that a humorist can have is to get your stuff into the Congressional Record. Just think, my name will be right in there along side of Huey Long's and all those other big humorists.

You see, ordinarily you got to work your way up as a humorist and first get into Congress. Then you work your way up into the Senate, and then, if your stuff is funny enough it goes into the Congressional Record. But for an outsider to get in there as a humorist without having served his apprenticeship in either the House or the Senate, why, mind you, I'm not bragging, but by golly I feel pretty big about it.

Did I ever tell you about the first time I ever had any stuff in that daily? Well, I'd written some fool thing, and it pertained to the bill that they were arguing—or that they were kidding about, rather—at the time in the Senate. So some Senator read my little article, and as it was during his speech, it naturally went into the Congressional Record. So another Senator rose and said, you know how they always do, if you ever seen 'em.

"Does the gentleman yield?" They always say "gentleman" in there. But the tone—the tone that they put on the word, it would be more appropriate— you know the way they can say "gentleman"—it would sound right if they come right out and said "Does the coyote from Maine yield?" You know what I mean; that's about the way it sounds. So the coyote from Maine says, "I yield to the polecat from Oregon," for if he don't, the other guy will keep on talking anyhow. You know he don't say "polecat," but he says "gentleman" in such a way that it's almost like polecat. They are very polite in there.

Well, I must get back to my story. When this senator read my offering, the other senator said (after all the yielding was all over) "I object! I object to the remarks of a professional jokemaker being put into the Record!" You know, meaning me. See? Taking a dig at me. They didn't want any outside fellow contributing. Well, he had me all wrong - compared to them, I'm an amateur! And the thing about my jokes is, they don't hurt anybody. You can take 'em or leave 'em - you can say they're funny or they're terrible or they're good, or whatever, but you can just pass 'em by. But with Congress, everytime they make a joke, it's a law! And every time they make a law, it's a joke!"

The Death of Charles Russell

Shortly after his friend of many years, renowned "cowboy artist" Charles Russell, passed away in 1926, Rogers wrote this farewell letter his friend and sent it to Russell's widow, Nancy.

Dear Charley,

I bet you hadn't been up there three days until you had out your pencil and was drawin' something funny. And I bet you that a whole bunch of those great old joshers was just a waitin' for you to pop in with all the latest ones.

And I bet they are regular fellows when you meet 'em, ain't they? Most big men are.

Well, you will run into my old Dad up there, Charley, for he was a real cowhand, and I bet he's runnin' a wagon. And you will pop into some well-kept ranchhouse over under some cool shade trees, and you will be asked to dinner, and it will be the best one you ever had in your life. Well, when you are thankin' the women folks you just tell the sweet lookin' little old lady that you knew her boy, back on an outfit you used to rope for, and tell the daughters that you knew their brother, and if you see a cute little rascal runnin' around there with my brand on him, kiss him for me.

Well, can't write any more, Charley, paper's all wet, it must be raining in this old bunkhouse.

From your old friend,

Will

Henry Ford for President

Will Rogers said of Henry Ford: *It will take a hundred years to know whether he helped us our hurt us, but he certainly didn't leave us where he found us.* Those feelings didn't stop Rogers from jokingly nominating his friend for president in a toast in 1923. He later followed up that toast with a Victor 78 recording and a mention in his newspaper column.

Here is a transcription of that recording followed by the newspaper column.

Will Rogers Nominates Henry Ford for President

Toastmasters, gentleman and you, too, politicians:

The Democrats are the Middle of the Road Party.

The Republicans are the Straddle of the Road Party.

So, I hereby nominate Mr. Henry Ford for President and christen the party" the All Over the Road Party.

In the first place it is too bad that he is too competent. That is the only thing that will beat him.

Mr. Ford's a good friend of mine and years ago he overlooked the suggestion that would have made him immortal. When he went over to stop the war, I wanted him to take the girls we had in The Follies and let them wear the same costumes they wore in the show. And march them down between the trenches ... believe me, the boys would've been out before Christmas. He has made more money than any man in the world by paying the highest wages. Yet he don't even manufacture a necessity. Neither would you call it a luxury ... it just kinda comes under the heading of "Nick-Nack".

I was at his home last year and happened to ask him that in case of stiff opposition just how cheap he could sell his cars. He said, "Why, Will, by controlling the selling of the parts, I could give the cars away." He said, "Why those things would shake off enough bolts in a year to pay for themselves. The second year, that's just pure profit."

People think Doctor Coué was the originator of auto suggestion, but Ford is. He originated auto suggestion, when he made this an option for the car. He just recently lowered the price $50. That's done to discourage thievery. He's the first man that ever took a joke and make it practical, so let's let him take this country. Maybe he can repeat.

He should make a good political race. He carries two-thirds of this country now. There's no reason why there shouldn't be a Ford in the White House, they're everywhere else.
He's the only man that could make Congress earn their salaries. He would start a bill through and give each one something to tack on to it. When it come out, it would be ready to use.

He is the only man that when Congress started stalling, could lift up the hood and see what is the matter with it.
Some are against him because he don't know history. What we need in there is a man who can make history, not recite it.

Now, if Mr. Ford will just take another one of my suggestions, he can be elected. If he would just make one speech and say, "Voters, if I am elected, I would change the front on 'em."

From a 1923 newspaper column:

I launched a Ford for President movement. You see I am figuring on going in the Cabinet, as he will have to be like all of them and pay off his political debts with jobs. You see, all these other Cabinets are picked, not on ability, but what they have done for the Party. Well, we ain't going to have any party. It's to be called the "All over the Road Party" with Mr. Ford for leader. Our slogan will be "Come with Ford and you will at least get somewhere." I will probably have to be Secretary of State, although I don't think I could stand the round of Conferences. I think Vice President would be about my speed. Of course I do hate to stay hid that long because I like for people to know who I am, but if it looks best for the Party for me to be sacrificed, why, I would do it.

I would love to see Mr. Ford in there, really. I don't know who started the idea that a President must be a Politician instead of a Business man. A Politician can't run any other kind of business. So there is no reason why he can run the U. S. That's the biggest single business in the World. I just would love to see Mr. Ford, when Congress pulled one of those long stalls of theirs, going around and lifting up the hood and seeing what is the matter.

Well, that's all for Automobiles and Politics...

Will Rogers for Vice-President

In 1927, National Press Club considered Rogers as vice-presidential candidate on the Calvin Coolidge ticket in 1928 with NPC president Louis Ludlow's announcement: "Our idea was that Will would represent noise and the president would stand for silence. The president could throw the lariat and Will could throw the bull, and it would make a well-balanced ticket." Instead they "decided to appoint Mr. Rogers Congressman-at-Large for the United States of America, his duties being to roam over the country, pry into the state of the Union, check up on prohibition enforcement and report at regular intervals to the National Press Club."

The next day, August 28, 1927, in his syndicated newspaper column, Rogers wrote: "My first official duty as Congressman-at-Large, which was bestowed on me last night, is to change the library of the overhauled White House into a fishing pool. That's economy for the taxpayers." He signed the column: "Yours, Congressman-at-Large Hon. Rogers."

Rogers once said, *"The man with the best job in the country is the vice-president. All he has to do is get up every morning and say, 'How is the president?'"* Here he pokes fun at political job qualifications in his satirical bid to run for VP.

The following is one of the bravest statements made in a political decade. I just got off and held a caucus with myself, and said, somebody has got to be sacrificed for the sake of party harmony. I hereby and hereon put myself in nomination, and to save some other man being humiliated by having to put me in nomination, why, I will just nominate myself.

Here is a certificate to show that this is bona fide: "I, Dr. Isadore Moskowitz, of 234 East Mott Street, have examined the enclosed patient, Mr. Will Rogers, and find him to be of sound mind and body. (In fact, sounder in body than mind.) This certifies that if he wants to run for Vice-President, I see no way of preventing it-(Signed) Isadore Moskowitz, Horse doctor's commission expires June 1, 1925."

So I, Will Rogers, of Claremore, Oklahoma, Hollywood, California, and Forty-Second Street and Broadway, New York, do hereby step right out and declare myself not only as a receptive, but anxious candidate for the second position on the forthcoming ticket.

Now on first hearing this, it might sound like a joke, but when I relate to you some of the qualifications which I possess, why, I think any fair-minded man will give me serious consideration. But the trouble is there are no fair-minded men in politics.

In the first place, they have got to nominate a farmer who understands the farmer's condition. Well, I got two farms in Oklahoma, both mortgaged, so no man knows their condition better than I do! He also has to be a man from the West. Well, if a man came from 25 feet further west than I lived last year, he would have to be a fish in the Pacific Ocean.
Another big reason why I should be nominated is that I am not a Democrat. Another, still bigger reason why I should be nominated is that I am not a Republican. I am just progressive

enough to suit the dissatisfied, and lazy enough to be a standpatter.

Oil has never touched me. The reason I know it never has, I drilled a well on my farm in Oklahoma and never even touched oil, much less oil touching me. I never worked for a big corporation.

When the President can't go anywhere, why, the Vice-President has got to go speak or eat for him. Now I could take in all the dinners, for I am a fair eater. I could say, "I am sorry the President can't come but he has pressing business." Of course, I wouldn't tell the real reason why he didn't come. So, you see, I am just a good enough liar to be a good Vice-President.

I am not much of an after-dinner speaker but I could learn two stories; one for dinners where ladies were present, and one for where they were not. Of course, I have no dress suit. The government would have to furnish me a dress suit. If I went to a dinner in a rented one, they would mistake me for a Congressman.

It won't take much to launch my campaign. We will wait and when some dark, or light, horse is eliminated, we will take their headquarters and buy their buttons and badges cheap. I can hear a lot of you all say, "Yes, Will, you would make a good Vice-President, but suppose something happened to the President?"

Well, I would do just like Mr. Coolidge. I would go in there and keep still and do nothing.

P.S. I was born in a log cabin.

Hoof-and-Mouth Disease

Rogers ridiculed the US government's action/inaction on an epidemic of hoof-and-mouth disease. When the government acted upon this situation, while remaining passive in related ones, he called out the government for ineptness and its waste of time and money, the last line being:

"Why can't we get a government to at least do for a child's protection, what they do for a cow?"

This letter was written a few years after his twenty-month-old son Fred died of Diphtheria when serum could not be supplied in time; although he never said it openly, he must have felt that appropriate government action could have saved his boy's life.

I am writing this out here in California and I don't know whether this will get through or not. We have an encounter out here with the hoof and mouth disease, and they are quarantining about everything that goes out of the state. Arizona is the worst; they tried to stop an aviator the other day that was flying over the state from California to Texas.

They don't allow passengers that are going through the state to get off the train. They have to carry the disease, if they have it, on into New Mexico. Of course, if they don't care to get off there, they can go on into Kansas or Oklahoma with it. They stopped a shipment of furniture; guess they figured that a cow might have occupied one of the beds at some time or another.

You see, a cloven hoofed animal is the only one that gets it. They get it first by breaking out between the slit part of their foot; then they lick it and it infects their mouth. That's where it derives its name, the foot and mouth disease.

Now with animals, when a case breaks out they shoot every animal of that same kind in the state.

You see this disease started a hundred years ago somewhere in Europe and they didn't know what it was; so the veterinarian just shot the cow and as there happened to be another cow standing by this one, and he happened to have two bullets, why, he shot her too.

Well, things went along until finally another case was discovered, and this veterinarian says to himself, "I will not only see them but raise them." So he shot the afflicted cow, then shot all of her friends. So that's the way this disease has drifted just from one shooting to another.

It's the only disease in the world where shooting is the remedy. Instead of developing veterinarians' medical knowledge, it has only developed their marksmanship. The U.S. Government appropriated one and one-half million dollars just for more ammunition to help eradicate the disease. The whole state has been put under federal marksmanship.

They have put an embargo on fruit and vegetables being shipped. Now if there is a man living that can tell me when a cabbage has the foot and mouth disease, and where, I will gladly retract. I don't care if carrots do have it; I hate them anyway.

Now they could find out something about how the disease works, but the minute it breaks out, why, they call a conference and they all get together and decide where the next conference will be. Then the next day they hold another conference.

If doctors of humans held that many conferences, everybody in the United States would die while they were conferring.

You wire the state or the federal government that your cow is sick and they will send out experts from Washington and appropriate money to eradicate the cause. You wire your government that your baby has the diphtheria or scarlet fever, and see what they do. All you will do is hire your own doctor, if you are able.

You can have 5 children down with infantile paralysis, more deadly 10 times over than any foot and mouth disease, and see how many doctors they send out from Washington to help you.

. . .Why can't we get a government to at least do for a child's protection, what they do for a cow?

US President Woodrow Wilson

Rogers maintained that Woodrow Wilson was the first US President to support his act, and wrote the following after the Wilson's death on February 3, 1924:

Some of the most glowing and deserving tributes ever paid to the memory of an American have been paid in the last few days to our past President Woodrow Wilson. They have been paid by learned men of this and all nations, who knew what to say and how to express their feelings. They spoke of their close association and personal contact with him. Now I want to add my little mite even though it be of no importance.

I want to speak and tell of him as I knew him, for he was my friend. We of the stage know that our audiences are our best friends, and he was the greatest audience of any public man we ever had. I want to tell of him as I knew him across the footlights. A great many actors and professional people have appeared before him, on various occasions in wonderful high class endeavors, but I don't think that any person met him across the footlights in exactly the personal way that I did on five different occasions.

Every other performer or actor did before him exactly what they had done before other audiences on the night previous. But I gave a great deal of time and thought to an act for him, most of which would never be used again, and had never been used before. Owing to the style of act I used, my stuff depended a great deal on what had happened that particular day or week. It just seemed by an odd chance for me every time I played before President Wilson that on that particular day there had been something of great importance that he had just been dealing with, for you must remember that each day was a day of great stress with him. He had no easy days. So when I could go into a theatre and get laughs out of our president, by poking fun at some turn in our national affairs, I don't mind telling you it was the happiest moment of my entire career on the stage.

The first time I shall never forget, for it was the most impressive and for me the most nervous one of them all. The Friars Club of New York, one of the biggest theatrical social clubs in New York, had decided to make a whirlwind tour of the principal cities of the East all in one week. We played a different city every night. We made a one night stand out of Chicago and New York. We were billed for Baltimore but not for Washington. President Wilson came over from Washington to see the performance. It was the first time in theatrical history that the president of the United States would be coming over to Baltimore just to see a comedy show.

It was at that time that we were having our little set-to with Mexico, and when we were at the height of our note exchanging career with Germany and Austria. The house was packed with the elite of Baltimore.

The show was going great. It was a collection of clever skits, written mostly by our stage's greatest man, George M. Cohan, and even down to the minor bits was played by stars with big reputations. I was the least known member of the entire aggregation, doing my little specialty with a rope, and telling jokes on national affairs, just a very ordinary little vaudeville act by chance sandwiched in among this great array.

I was on late and as the show went along I would walk out of the stage door and out on the street and try to kill time and nervousness until it was time to dress and go on. I had never told jokes to a president, much less about one, especially to his face. Well, I am not kidding you when I tell you that I was scared to death. I am always nervous. I never saw an audience that I ever faced with any confidence, for no man can ever tell how a given audience will ever take anything.

But here I was, nothing but an ordinary Oklahoma cow-puncher who had learned to spin a rope a little and who had learned to read the daily papers a little, going out before the aristocracy of Baltimore, and the president of the United States, and kid about some of the policies with which he was shaping the destinies of nations.

How was I to know but what the audience would rise up in mass and resent it. I had never heard, and I don't think anyone else had ever heard of a president being joked personally in a public theater about the policies of his administration.
The nearer the time came the worse scared I got. George M. Cohan and others, knowing how I felt, would pat me on the back and tell me, "Why, he is just a human being; go on out and do your stuff." Well, if somebody had come through the dressing room and hollered "Train for Clare-more, Oklahoma, leaving at once" I would have been on it. This all may sound strange but any who have had the experience know that a presidential appearance in a theater, especially outside Washington, D.C., is a very rare and unique feeling even to the audience. They are keyed up almost as much as the actors.

At the time of his entrance into the house, everybody stood up and there were plain clothes men all over the place, back stage and behind his box. How was I to know but what one of them might not take a shot at me if I said anything about him personally?

Finally a warden knocked at my dressing room door and said, "You die in 5 more minutes for kidding your country." They just literally shoved me out on the stage.

Now, by a stroke of what I call good fortune, (for I will keep them always), I have a copy of the entire acts that I did for President Wilson on the five times I worked for him. My first remark in Baltimore was, "I am kinder nervous here tonight." Now that is not an especially bright remark, and I don't hope to go down in history on the strength of it, but it was so apparent to the audience that I was speaking the truth that they laughed heartily at it. After all, we all love honesty.

Then I said, "I shouldn't be nervous, for this is really my second presidential appearance. The first time was when William Jennings Bryan spoke in our town once, and I was to follow his speech and do my little roping act." Well, I heard them laughing, so I took a sly glance at the president's box and sure enough he was laughing just as big as anyone. So I went on. "As I say, I was to follow him, but he spoke so long that it was so dark when he finished they couldn't see my roping." That went over great, so I said, "I wonder what ever become of him?" That was all right, it got over, but still I had made no direct reference to the president.

Now General Pershing was in Mexico at the time, and there was a lot in the papers for and against the invasion. I said, "I see where they have captured Pancho Villa. Yes, they got him in the morning editions and then the afternoon ones let him get away." Now everybody in the house before they would laugh looked at the president, to see how he was going to take it. Well, he started laughing and they all followed suit.

"Villa raided Columbus, New Mexico. We had a man on guard that night at the post. But to show you how crooked this Villa is, he sneaked up on the opposite side." "We chased him over the line 5 miles, but run into a lot of government red tape and had to come back." "There is some talk of getting a machine gun if we can borrow one. . . . The one we have now they are using to train our army with in Plattsburgh. ... if we go to war we will just about have to go to the trouble of getting another gun."

Now mind you, he was being rode on all sides for our lack of preparedness, yet he sat there and led that entire audience in laughing at the ones on himself. At that time there was talk of forming an army of 2 hundred thousand men. So I said, "We are going to have an army of 2 hundred thousand men. Mr. Henry Ford makes 3 hundred thousand cars a year. I think, Mr. President, we ought to at least have a man to every car. . . . See where they got Villa hemmed in between the Atlantic and Pacific. Now all we got to do is to stop up both ends."

"Pershing located him at a town called Los Quas Ka Jasbo. Now all we have to do is locate Los Quas Ka Jasbo."

"I see by a headline that Villa escapes net and flees. We will never catch him then. Any Mexican that can escape fleas is beyond catching. . . . But we are doing better toward preparedness now, as one of my senators from Oklahoma has sent home a double portion of garden seed."

After various other ones on Mexico I started in on European affairs which at that time was long before we entered the war.

"We are facing another crisis tonight, but our president here has had so many of them lately that he can just lay right down and sleep beside one of those things."

Then I first pulled the one which I am proud to say he afterwards repeated to various friends as the best one told on him during the war. I said, "President Wilson is getting along fine now to what he was a few months ago. Do you realize, people, that at one time in our negotiating with Germany that he was 5 notes behind?"

How he did laugh at that! Well, due to him being a good fellow and setting a real example, I had the proudest and most successful night I ever had on the stage. I had lots of gags on other subjects but the ones on him were the heartiest laughs with him, and so it was on all the other occasions I played for him. He come backstage at intermission and chatted and shook hands with all.

Some time I would like to tell of the things he laughed at during the most serious stages of the great war. What he stood for and died for will be strived after for years. But it will take time, for with all our advancement and boasted civilization, it's hard to stamp out selfishness and greed. For after all, nations are nothing but individuals, and you can't stop even brothers from fighting sometimes.

But he helped it along a lot. And what a wonderful cause to have laid down your life for. The world lost a friend. The theater lost its greatest supporter. And I lost the most distinguished person who ever laughed at my little nonsensical jokes, I looked forward to it every year. Now I have only to look back on it as my greatest memory."

Prohibition

In 1919, Rogers wrote a book: "The Cowboy Philosopher on Prohibition"; in 1930 he wrote the following telegram to the Washington Post about the "wets" and the "drys" [the "drys" are those who favor prohibition; the "wets" are those who are against prohibition]. Following the telegram is the transcription of a radio broadcast in which Rogers skewers both sides of the Prohibition issue, coaxing the zealots on both sides of the debate to move toward a less hard line position.

Draft of Telegram to Editor, *Washington Post*
8 June 1930
[New York, NY]

Editor Washington Post.
Washington, DC.

I HEREBY OFFER MY SERVICES TO PROHIBITION INVESTIGATION?
I WANT TO TESTIFY IN BEHLF OF THE PEOPLE OF AMERICA WHO ARE TIERED
OF LISTENING TO BOTH SIDES? AND WANT TO BE LET ALONE? EIGHTY PERECNT
OF AMERICA WISH THAT THE WETS WOULD GET SO DRUNK THEY WOULD BE
SPEECHLESS FOR THE REST OF THEIR LIVES. AND THE DRYS GET SO ~~PERFCCT~~

PERFECT THAT THEY WOULD BE CALLED AWAY
TO HEAVAN/ THEN WHAT A WON-
DERFUL PLACE IT WOULD BE FOR THE REST OF
AMERICA TO LIVE IN.
THIS ARGUMENT IS JUST LIKE A WAR??IT'S THE
INNOCENT THAT SUFFER.

In Behalf of Humanity,
Will Roegrs.

I have received more letters in the last few weeks to talk on
Prohibition than on any other subject. I haven't said a word
about it. I was really ashamed. So many was talking and
arguing over it that I wanted to be original and just let it alone.
Can you name me one subject in the entire world that there
has been as much time and energy wasted on?...

I have often said that I wish the wets would become so soused
they would be speechless and couldn't say anything, and that
the drys would become so perfect that the Lord would come
down and take them away from here—and that would leave the
country to the rest of us who are tired of listening to both of
them. So I got to wondering if it wasn't possible for a fellow to
talk on it without being a nut on the other side. I think if I
could do that I would be speaking in behalf of practically
millions of people.

Now it is not so terribly serious, this Prohibition. It is not a
life-or-death problem with us. If it was repealed tomorrow, the
lives and habits and morals of the whole country they wouldn't
be ruined; the country would drag along just the same. Taxes
and parking spaces would hit us in the face just the same.

Henry Ford wouldn't leave the country if it was repealed—you couldn't run him out of here.

Then, on the other hand, if it is never repealed, we will still drag along. The country won't go to the dogs. We lived with the Eighteenth Amendment and we have lived without it, and we are still here under both systems. So you see there is perhaps problems greater.... America is getting so big—you know, it really is, this country is getting so big—that no matter what it is, it don't bother us anymore. We just struggle along in spite of ourselves. It takes more than a drink to really interest us anymore. It is not undermining the moral fiber of a great nation. That's a lot of hooey [nonsense]....

Some folks on both sides have just kidded themselves it is our greatest problem. The real wet is going to drink, I don't care what your laws are, and a real dry is going to lecture to him while he is drinking, no matter what your laws about it are. You can't change human nature. But while those two are fighting it out, there will be five hundred passing by tending to their own business, living their own lives, and doing exactly what they think is best for them....

We are trying to settle something here that has been going on since way back in Bible times. Those old prophets couldn't even settle it, and you can't tell me that Moses of New Hampshire [Republican and Prohibitionist Senator George Higgins] and his gang of senators know any more than Moses of Palestine and his troop did. Right in the first book of Genesis [first book of the Bible], you don't read but just a few pages until Noah was lit up like a pygmy golf course. Here is just how it started—wait a minute, I got it right here on paper—I will read it to you. Right in the start of Genesis, the ninth chapter and twentieth verse, it says, "And Noah became a husbandman and planted a vineyard." The minute he became a husband he started in raising the ingredients that goes with married life. So you can trace all drink to marriage, see. What we got to prohibit is marriage. In the very next verse, the twenty—first verse, it says, "And he drank of the wine and was drunk." Now that was Noah himself, our forefather. Practically all of us can trace our ancestry back to him....

Now you see Noah drank and he didn't drink water, and he was a man that knew more about water than practically any man of his time. He was the water commissioner of his day.

Old Noah was an expert on water, but the Lord is very far-seeing, and everything He does is for the best. Through Noah partaking of too much wine and going on his little spree, that is just why the Lord picked on him to pick out these animals to take into the Ark—he was the only man that had even seen all of them. So if Noah hadn't drunk, today we would be without circuses and menageries Of course, other men since Noah's time have claimed that they have seen animals that Noah didn't put into the Ark—but they were drinking from a different vineyard....

Noah lived—you know this wine had such ill effects on Noah that he only lived to be 950 years old. That is just nineteen years short of Methuselah, who held the longevity record of his and all times. So Prohibition is not a new problem by any means. There is no need for this generation to feel conceited enough to think that they can settle it. It is like stopping war. We are always going to want to do something that no other generation had ever been able to do. If you could take politics out of Prohibition, it would be more beneficial to this country than if you took the alcohol out of our drinks.

America ain't as bad off as it might seem. The young are not drinking themselves to death and the old are not worrying themselves to death over the condition of whether the young are drinking or not. Chain stores are worrying this country a lot more than chain saloons are. Turkey is the only other Prohibition country in the world, us and Turkey. There's a fine gang to be linked up with, ain't it? If we enjoyed some of the other privileges, things wouldn't be so bad. We enjoy them, but they are not legal.

Now listen here, folks—honest, this is what I want to get over to you tonight. Let's not all get excited about it and break friendships with our neighbors and fall out with our brother over this Prohibition. Nothing is going to be done about it during our lifetime. There ain't anybody hearing me tonight who will live to see the time when anything is done about it, so don't let's all worry and get all het' up [heated up] about it, get all hot and bothered. Don't let's take it so serious. The drys and wets both combined can't hurt this country. Talking about Prohibition is like whittling used to be: It passes away the time but don't settle anything.

Now go to bed and forget about it, and let's hope that someday our country will be as dry as the speeches made by both the wets and the drys....

Rogers' Last Words

On August 15, 1935, Rogers was flying with famed aviator Wiley Post near Point Barrow, Alaska when their plane crashed, killing both of them. One of his last acts was giving Joe Crosson (a well-known Alaskan bush pilot who flew the bodies of Rogers and Post to Seattle from Barrow, Alaska) a telegram to his daughter Mary, who was playing in summer stock in Maine:

> "Great Trip. Wish you were all along. How's your acting? You and Mama wire me all the news to Nome. Going to Point Barrow today. Furthest point on land on whole American continent. Lots of Love, Don't Worry, "Dad"

The following article was in progress at the time of the accident and was found aboard the plane. It was not released until several years after it was written.

[UNTITLED]

Well all I know about dogs is not much, but when I was up in Alaska there is an awful lot of dependence put in dogs, not enough to untie one from a chain, but theyrs whole existence tangles around dogs, of course the plane has diminished the dog travel a lot but still backbone of the Arctic is a dog's backbone. I met up there just as I was leaving Fairbanks that famous "Musher" and dog race winner, "Seppala," he become immortal on that famous drive with the infantile paralysis serum to Nome. Well I dident have long to talk to him that morning, as we was trying to get off, and the river was soret narrow and many bends and Wiley was afraid that in it with a full load of gas that we might have some difficulty in taking off, so we had some gas sent out to a lake about 50 miles out, and then flew there and loaded up and took off, we were headed at the time for Point Barrow the furtherest north of any piece of land on the North American Continent, (there is island in the Arctic, but no land on the mainland further north). It was over an entirely uninhabited country, only we did get over that little village of Wiseman, did you ever read the book "The Arctic Village," well I must tell you about it some time. It was very popular and best sellar, and the author lived there a year or more and uses all the people in the town and their names right in the book. I got it and am reading it and will tell you about it, but to get back to Seppala and too dogs, for Seppala is as identified with dogs as May West is with buxomness.

He has a splendid book written with him by Elizabeth Ricker who herself is a great dog fancier and dog driver. Well not knowing anything about it, I asked him about the dog "Balto" that there is now a statue too in Central Park New York in honor of this great race, and he told me. Balto was not the dog, the real hero of the race was "Togo" my lead dog, Balto was not in my team, he was in the team of the driver who made the last lap or entry into Nome, and hence he received all the credit, and Balto was not even the lead dog, the newspaper men asked him the names of the dogs and the driver told them the leader was "Fox." Well half the dog teams in the North they said was named Fox, so they kept asng other dogs names in the team, and finally he mentioned "Balto" so they hopped on that right away it had headline possibilitys, and today I guess all over the world you find it on dog food boxes. The run out to meet the serum coming in wasent originally to be done in relays by different teams, they had asked him to go out some 300 miles out and that far back, to get it, and he picked his best dogs, 20 of them for the trip, meaning to leave some along the line to use on his way back after he had gotten the serum, but after he left the disease spread and they had it started from the other end. And he met it 170 miles out instead of the 300, then he made the run with it through a terrible storm but a relay team met him. But in all he had covered over 300 miles going or coming for the serum, and no other driver had made over 53 miles. He said he dident mind it for himself but that it was his wonderful lead dog "Fox" that did such great work and then lost the credit. Balto he had raised as well as Fox, and he had left Balto at home as he was a dog that he used on just his freight team. He used to win most all those big dog races, the biggest of which was the "Alaskan Sweepstakes," which had prizes as high as $20.000.

He is a little bit of a fellow, but mighty husky. He works for a big mining company in Fairbanks. He has charge of a section of big water line, a pipe line about six feet in diameter that runs for over a 100 miles. It has burst when we was there and we had drove out to see it. He said he might get back in the racing game, but that he was I believe he said 58 years old. Kinder said it like he thought a man that age better be dying off, and it dident make me feel any too chipper. One of the hardest things he said is to train dog teams to pass on the trail and not go to war with each other. Then you are all winter separating 'em, to say nothin of how long it takes to seperate the drivers. They don't drive the big long teams as much as they used too, for they don't have the big loads. They used to hitch 18 or 20. Now 4 or 6 or 8. Joe Crosson the ace pilot that we were with so much in Fairbanks an old friend of Wiley's, he has a mine and we went out there, and he has a partner a Swedish fellow that runs it and he had just killed a bear right at his house door. And the Sweedish fellow tells how Mickey went out one night and run the bear in. Well as a matter of fact

Mickey went out and the bear chased him in, and Earnest had to shoot the bear to keep him from running Mickey under the bed. They say there is more fellows been caught by a bear just that way. An old pet dog, (Mickey is a wirehaired fox terrier) jumps the bear and then they hike straight to you, and the bear after 'em, and the first thing you know you got a bear in your lap, and a dog between your feet. So "Mickey" is a great bear dog. So there is two kinds of bear dogs the ones that drive 'em away and the ones that bring 'em in. Little Mickey thought he had done it, as Earnest said he chewed all the hair off the bear, after death. Now I must get back to advising my Democrats.

THE "WORDS & WISDOM" SERIES

Available from Amazon.com and other retailers

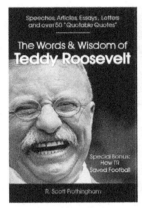

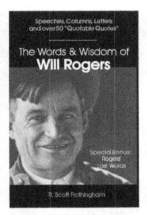

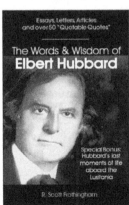

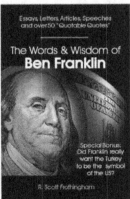

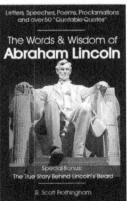

Selections of the actual words of historical figures
that will give you a better understanding of
the people behind the beloved icons and notable events.

ABOUT THE AUTHOR

Scott Frothingham is an entrepreneur, consultant, speaker, business coach and author best known for his FastForward Income™ products including *The 15-minute Sales Workout*™. He helps entrepreneurs, managers and sales/marketing executives position themselves for success through skills training and personal development -- along with providing tools for effectively and efficiently training and motivating their teams.

R. Scott Frothingham

www.ScottFrothingham.com

Facebook: **www.Facebook.com/FastForwardIncome**

Twitter: **@ScottFroth**

www.FastForwardPublishing.com

Edward S. Ellis is best known for his youth-targeted fictional works in the American dime, pulp, and series novel genre like *Seth Jones* or *The Captives of the Frontier* (described as the "perfect dime novel" of thrilling frontier adventure -- estimated 60,000 copies in its first week and 450,000 copies in its first six months), *The Huge Hunter* or *The Steam Man of the Prairies* (first U.S. science fiction dime novel) and the series featuring Native American: Deerfoot. Later in life he turned to more serious work, writing acco unts of historical events and biographies, mostly for adults.

For more details on the life, career and books of Edward S. Ellis, visit **www.EdwardSEllis.com**.

www.FastForwardPublishing.com

Made in the USA
Las Vegas, NV
19 August 2022

53566521R00056